HISTORY

Facts You Won't Believe!

HUGH WESTRUP

interior illustrations
by Robert Roper

ISBN 0-439-14703-4

Text copyright © 1999 by Scholastic Inc. Illustrations copyright © 1999 by Scholastic Inc.
All rights reserved. Published by Scholastic Inc.

SCHOLASTIC and associated logos are trademarks and/or registered trademarks of Scholastic Inc.

12 11 10 9 8 7 6 5 4   3 4/0

Printed in the U.S.A.   01

First Scholastic printing, October 1999

TABLE OF CONTENTS

Acknowledgments

The author would like to thank Oneil Cormier, Fran Downey, and Stephen Fraser for their assistance and advice.

Human beings, scientists tell us, have been on earth for two million years. Most of that time is known as prehistory. Only about 5,000 years ago, humans advanced to the point where they began writing things down in books, diaries, letters, and other documents. The first such scratchings marked the beginning of history.

Though 5,000 years isn't long, enough history has been written in that time to fill entire libraries. This book is a tiny sampling of what lies in those libraries — a pinkie toe dipped into the pool of past human events.

I hope you enjoy the plunge.

NOTE

Historians use the terms B.C. and A.D. to indicate when events took place. The term B.C. means *before Christ*. An event that happened in 300 B.C. happened 300 years before the birth of Jesus Christ. The term A.D. means *anno Domini*, which is Latin for "in the year of our Lord." An event that happened in A.D. 300 happened 300 years after the birth of Christ. All the dates in this book took place *anno Domini* except when designated B.C.

- The first civilization on earth was the Sumerian civilization. It arose about 5,500 years ago (3500 B.C.) in a region that is now part of Iraq. The Sumerians gave the world writing, arithmetic, schools, irrigation, and the first kings, among other things.

- When a Sumerian king died, his entire household of seventy or so people killed themselves with poison in order to follow him into the afterlife.

- The oldest story in the world is the *Epic of Gilgamesh*, which the Sumerians first wrote down about 4,000 years ago. It is an epic poem that tells of a great flood in which only one family survives by building an ark. Does that remind you of another famous flood story?

- Judaism is the world's oldest major religion. It was founded about 4,000 years ago by Abraham. The religion took its name from Judah, one of Abraham's great-grandsons.

- The Assyrians, who lived in what is now northern Iraq, were very hair-conscious. Assyrian beauticians were masters at cutting, curling, oiling, dyeing, and perfuming hair. A stylist who gave a bad haircut could be sentenced to death.

HALF PRICE?

- People today buy soda and candy bars from coin-operated machines. In the ancient Egyptian city of Alexandria, people put bronze coins into machines that dispensed holy water required for washing the face and hands before entering a temple.

- History's first known written advertisement was a "Wanted" poster put up 3,000 years ago in the Egyptian city of Thebes. It offered the reward of a gold coin for the return of a runaway slave named Shem.

- In 1000 B.C., the Israelites paid their taxes with raisins.

- Polygamy is a marriage in which a man has two or more wives at the same time. It was common in many ancient societies. In the Bible, Solomon is said to have had 200 wives.

- The ancient Egyptians regarded cats as holy animals. When a pet cat died, it was mummified, and its owners went into mourning and shaved their eyebrows.

- The first Olympic games took place in Greece in 776 B.C. All athletes performed naked and only men were allowed to compete. Women could not participate or even watch.

- A woman in ancient Greece counted her age not from birth but from the date of her marriage.

- Cosmetics were popular with both men and women in the ancient world of the Mediterranean. Even the men of Greece, who did not use facial makeup, doused their bodies with perfumes. They put mint perfume on their arms, cinnamon perfume on their chests, and almond perfume on their hands and feet.

- Nike, the modern sports gear manufacturer, took its name from Nike, the ancient Greek goddess of victory.

- Democracy began about 500 B.C. in the Greek city of Athens. Though women and slaves were not allowed to vote, every man had the duty of serving in the Assembly, which passed laws and made important decisions.

- Herodotus (477–431 B.C.) was a historian who lived in the Golden Age of ancient Greece. He has been called the Father of History and wrote many colorful accounts of Greece's war with Persia.

- The Scythians were barbarians who lived in what is now Russia. According to Herodotus, the Scythians beheaded their enemies and used the skulls as drinking cups.

- The ancient Romans smeared pigeon poop in their hair. Pigeon poop contains the chemical ammonia, which bleaches hair.

- The Romans did not practice their religion in public. Religious worship took place at home, where the entire household gathered at a private altar to worship images that represented dead relatives.

- Queen Cleopatra VII (69–30 B.C.) was the last ruler of Egypt before it was conquered by the Romans. She wore a fake beard when she presided over court functions to show that she could be as strong as a man.

- The Gauls of ancient France had a unique long-distance communication system. Long before telephones were invented, farmers shouted the news from one field to the next. An urgent piece of news could travel more than 150 miles in a single day that way.

- The custom of having a best man at a wedding began about 2,000 years ago in northern Europe. When a man wanted to marry, he sometimes kidnapped a woman from a nearby village. To help the man capture and keep the woman, a male friend — the "best man" — would often come along.

- Christmas was not celebrated until 400 years after Jesus Christ. No one knows the exact birth date of Christ. Christmas was observed at the end of December because that was the time of year that people held festivals to celebrate the arrival of the winter solstice — the lengthening of days and the return of light and life.

- Easter was named after Eastre, a goddess of the Saxon people, who lived in northern Europe. Eastre's symbol was the rabbit, from which came the Easter bunny.

- Kissing did not become widely accepted in Europe as a sign of affection until about 500.

- The Middle Ages of Europe, otherwise known as the medieval period, began after the fall of the Roman Empire late in the 5th century.

- In the Middle Ages, the Roman Catholic Church became the most powerful organization in Europe.

- People were dirty and smelly during the Middle Ages in Europe because bathing was considered unhealthy.

- Childhood during the medieval period was different from what it is today. Children were considered tiny adults. Instead of going to school, medieval kids went out into the world to work, compete, and play with adults.

- The emperor Charlemagne (742–814) had the heads of 4,500 people chopped off in one morning because they refused to be baptized into the Christian church.

- Many pagan (a belief in many gods) customs survived during the Middle Ages. A famous medieval stone cross that still stands in northern England is carved with the figures of Jesus Christ and many Viking gods, including the evil god Loki and the supreme god Woden.

- The expression "to give the cold shoulder" means to be unfriendly. It began in the Middle Ages when household guests who had overstayed their welcome were served a shoulder of cold beef.

- Once a year in medieval France, the country's churches and cathedrals were the scenes of wild parties. Dressed in costumes, masks, and flowers, the partyers feasted, sang, danced, and gambled on their annual Feast of Fools.

- From 950 to 1300, the Northern Hemisphere was much warmer than it is today. That extra warmth melted many icebergs and made the water warmer in the north Atlantic Ocean. It helped the Viking explorer Leif Eriksson cross the north Atlantic 1,000 years ago and become the first European to reach North America.

- When a Viking died far from home, his mates boiled his body until only his bones were left. The bones would then be carried home in a box.

- Hanging women criminals or burning them at the stake was thought to be indecent in northern Europe in medieval times. Instead, the women were buried alive.

- In the Middle Ages, people blew their noses with their fingers.

- During the Middle Ages, pigs were sometimes tried for murder. Most of the pigs' victims were small children who had been left to play near the pigs by careless parents. The pigs were tortured and, if found guilty, made into pork chops.

- Musical harmony began during the Middle Ages. Before then, musicians followed just one simple melody line.

- In the 13th century, the word "girl" meant any young person, male or female.

- Throughout most of the Middle Ages, people were known by only one name. When second names were adopted during the late Middle Ages, the names usually referred to a person's job or place of residence.

- Medieval pots and dishes were made of cheap clay called *pygg*. Housewives would put coins in clay jars and call them their pygg banks or pyggy banks. Years later, people forgot that pygg was a type of clay. Potters made earthenware banks shaped like actual pigs for customers who demanded pyggy banks.

PYGGY BANK
1252

PIGGY BANK
1999

- The Flagellants were people who lived in Germany, Flanders, and France in medieval times. They flogged themselves to a frenzy with metal-tipped whips to pay for their sins.

- During the Middle Ages, most people did not know in what year they were living or even in what year they were born.

- Hula hoops were a popular fad in the United States in the 1950s, but an earlier hula hoop craze swept Europe during the 14th century.

- In medieval times, poodles were kept as retrievers and had the job of fetching ducks and other waterbirds. The name poodle comes from an old German word, *pudel*, which is related in meaning to our word puddle.

- A frightening disease called Saint Vitus' dance, or tarantism, first appeared in 14th-century Europe. For hours or even days, victims of the disease leaped about uncontrollably, screaming furiously and foaming at the mouth. Modern doctors call the disease Sydenham's chorea.

- The modern word "slave" comes from the name "Slav." Slavs are people who belong to a number of groups that live mostly in Eastern Europe. During the 15th century, Italian merchants sold Slavs captured during wartime to wealthy families, who put the captives to work as servants.

- King Henry VIII (1491–1547) of England ordered the execution of 72,000 of his subjects. Some of his victims were boiled alive.

- Henry VIII's daughter, Queen Elizabeth I (1533–1603), was one of history's greatest rulers. She had black teeth that were rotten from eating too many sweets.

SAY, HOW'S ABOUT SOME CHOCOLATES?

- A craze called "tulipomania" swept Holland from 1634 to 1637. Tulips were rare then and many people tried to get rich by buying and selling tulip bulbs. One of the most precious bulbs was sold for $5,200.

- In 1655, the Marquis de Canillac watched his own execution from a hiding place nearby. People in France could be tried for crimes even if they hadn't been caught. If a missing person was sentenced to death, a dummy of that person would be made. The dummy would then be hung by a noose or its head chopped off.

- On December 5, 1664, a ship sank off the coast of Wales and the only survivor was a man named Hugh Williams. On the same date in 1785, another ship sank and the sole survivor was also a man named Hugh Williams. On the very same date in 1860, yet another ship sank and the one survivor was a man named — you've got it — Hugh Williams!

- Forks were not widely used in Europe until the 1700s. Before that, Europeans ate their meals with their fingers. One German priest went so far as to say that forks were instruments of the devil.

- Abandoned children were a common sight in Paris in the 16th and 17th centuries. Many poor people there could not afford to raise families and left their children on the street to be rescued and sent to hospitals for orphans.

- King Louis XIV (1638–1715) of France often conducted his affairs while sitting on the toilet.

- The people of England began using contractions such as can't, don't, and won't in the 17th century. One of those contractions was an't, which meant "am not" or "are not." Over the years, an't gained the letter "i" and became ain't.

- The custom of putting lost teeth under pillows for the tooth fairy probably came from Germany. German children put their lost teeth in mouse or rat holes hoping that their new teeth would grow in as strong as rodent choppers.

- Riots broke out in England in September 1752 when the government replaced the Julian calendar with the Gregorian calendar. People rioted because the change meant that September 3 suddenly became September 14, and eleven days were lost.

- Public hangings were popular during the Georgian period of British history (1714–1830). Grandstand tickets were sold for many hangings, and tens of thousand of spectators turned out to watch the most famous criminals be executed.

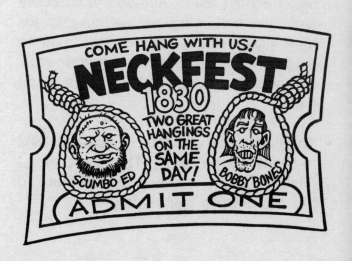

- The electric lightbulb was not invented by Thomas Edison. An Englishman, Sir Humphrey Davy (1778–1829), invented it in 1802. Edison improved on Davy's idea in 1879.

- European cities exploded in size during the 1800s because so many people migrated from the country to work in the new factories. The population of Berlin, Germany, grew from 170,000 in 1800 to 2.7 million in 1900.

- In 19th-century Paris, theater owners paid people called *claqueurs* to sit in the audience and whip up enthusiasm for their plays. Some people were paid to laugh at comedies, some to cry at dramas, and some to shout "Encore!" at a play's end.

- The first frankfurters were made in 1852 in Frankfurt, Germany. They were called dachshund sausages because they looked like the German weiner dog.

- In 1827, Parisians went wild over a new celebrity, the first living giraffe to visit France from Africa. Songs and poems were written about the magnificent animal, and her image was put on everything from toothpicks and purses to shaving bowls and gingerbread.

- From ancient times until the 20th century, respectable women in Europe (and America) never exposed their legs in public. Men, dressed in tunics and other short outfits, were the ones who showed off their shapely gams.

- Until the mid-1800s, medical surgery in Europe (and America) was a highly risky undertaking. Surgeons didn't know how to put patients to sleep during operations or prevent infections from developing after surgery. About half of all patients who had major surgery died from shock, pain, or infections.

- The 1800s was a century of rapid expansion for the empires of Europe. By the early 1900s, the European empires controlled about four-fifths of the world's land surface.

- The armies of the ancient world sometimes rode into battle on horses and
elephants outfitted in coats of metal
armor.

- King Cambyses of Persia won a war
against the Egyptian city of Memphis
in 525 B.C. by throwing cats over the walls
of the city. The ancient Egyptians
regarded cats as heavenly creatures, so
the people of Memphis were horrified
at the sight of cats being used as live
cannonballs. They quickly surrendered to
the Persians.

- The Servile War (73–71 B.C.) was a slave
rebellion led by a Roman gladiator named
Spartacus. One million slaves lived in
Italy at the time, and Spartacus organized
100,000 of them to fight the Roman army.
The slave army won some victories, but
the rebellion was finally crushed and
most of the slaves were killed.

- Giant mechanical claws once protected the ancient coastal city of Syracuse on the island of Sicily. When a foreign navy invaded the harbor, the giant claws would lift the ships, shake out the sailors, and then dash the boats against the rocks, smashing them to bits.

- In the summer of 410, barbarians broke through the walls of Rome with battering rams, then looted the city and murdered many inhabitants. The emperor Honorius (384–423) was away on vacation at the time. When informed that Rome had been destroyed, he mistakenly assumed someone had killed his pet chicken, also named Rome.

- Bees have often been used as weapons of war. King Richard I of England, Richard the Lionhearted (1157–1199), had his troops hurl beehives at their enemies.

- The Mongols were the most savage con-
querers in history, and their empire cov-
ered most of Asia in the late 1200s. In one
instance, the Mongol emperor Genghis
Khan (1167–1227) had his warriors kill all
but 50 of the 100,000 residents of the Per-
sian city of Nishapur.

- The Crusades were religious wars in
which Christians tried to recapture Pales-
tine, the birthplace of Jesus Christ, from
the Muslims. The most tragic Crusade
happened in 1212 when 50,000 children
left Europe by foot and by boat for the
Holy Land. Most of the children died on
the way or were captured and sold into
slavery.

- The Hundred Years War between France
and England really lasted 116 years —
from 1337 to 1453. It was a series of wars
interrupted by truces and treaties.

- The country of Japan has "nose tombs"
containing 20,000 noses that were cut
from the faces of Koreans and brought

home as trophies during a 16th-century Japanese invasion of Korea.

• The War of Jenkins' Ear (1739–1743) between Britain and Spain started when a Spanish patrol cut off the ear of an English shipmaster named Robert Jenkins while he was sailing in the West Indies.

- The Battle of Bunker Hill (1775) was the first major conflict of the American Revolution. It did not happen on Bunker Hill, however. It happened on nearby Breed's Hill, which was later renamed Bunker Hill.

- Robert Shurtleff was the only woman to fight in the American Revolution. Shurtleff's real name was Deborah Sampson (1760–1827), and she served in the army disguised as a man until she got sick and her superiors discovered that he was really a she.

- During the American Civil War (1861–1865), rich men paid poor men as much as $2,000 to fight in their place.

- A carrier pigeon named Cher Ami saved the lives of a group of American servicemen who were trapped by German soldiers during World War I (1914–1918).

Cher Ami carried a message from the soldiers through enemy fire to army headquarters. Though Cher Ami was hit twice by bullets and lost a leg and an eye, he delivered the message and was awarded a medal for bravery.

- The first jeep was built in 1940 by the Butler Car Company in response to a request by the U.S. Army for an all-purpose vehicle. The word jeep came from a Popeye cartoon in which a character named Jeep "could do almost everything."

- Old movie newsreels showing scenes of foreign wars were often faked because actual footage of the battles didn't look realistic enough. One newsreel that supposedly showed a Japanese attack on China was really filmed in New Jersey.

- The U.S. Marine Corps awarded a Purple Heart to a jeep that was "wounded" in a battle during World War II (1939–1945).

- During World War II, the U.S. Marine Corps recruited Navajo Indians to radio messages between units. Enemies who overheard the messages could not decode the messages because they didn't understand the Navajo language.

- Winston Churchill (1874–1965) is remembered for giving many great radio speeches as prime minister of Great Britain during World War II. Few people knew that an English actor named Norman Shelley actually delivered the speeches.

- Thirty-eight million people died during World War II — more than in any other war in history. World War II was also the most expensive war in history, costing $560 million.

- About 110,000 people were killed when the United States dropped atomic bombs on the Japanese cities of Hiroshima and Nagasaki during World War II. More people died, however, when American and British planes bombed the German city of Dresden during that war. The huge firestorm claimed about 135,000 lives.

- The first New England was not located in the northeastern United States. In the 1570s, the English explorer Sir Francis Drake (1543–1596) claimed a small slice of land in what is now California for Queen Elizabeth I. He called that piece of land New England.

- Christmas was outlawed in Massachusetts from 1659 to 1681. The Puritans considered Christmas a frivolous Roman Catholic celebration.

- Most American colonists did not support the American Revolution (1775–1783). Only about one third supported it. Another third supported the British and the remaining third did not care which side won.

- The American Revolution freed men of their wigs. Before the revolution, gentlemen shaved their heads and wore hot, heavy hairpieces. After the revolution, they let their hair grow into ponytails.

- The United States was declared independent on July 2, not July 4, 1776. The Fourth of July is celebrated as the anniversary of independence because that was the day that Thomas Jefferson finished writing the Declaration of Independence.

- The Liberty Bell in Philadelphia's Independence Hall has two flaws. The first one is its famous crack. The second one is a spelling mistake. Pennsylvania is spelled Pensylvania on the bell.

- Some historians say that the first president of the United States was John Hanson (1721–1783), not George Washington. Hanson was elected president of the U.S. Congress, which governed the country until 1789, the year the office of president was created and George Washington was elected to it.

- During the early years of the American republic, only wealthy landowners were allowed to vote. In an election held in 1787, only 4 percent of the U.S. population voted.

- In 1776, New Jersey gave men, women, poor people, and African-Americans the right to vote. Shortly after, the state's laws were changed and only white men who owned property were allowed to vote.

- Benjamin Franklin (1706–1790) did not want the bald eagle to be the national symbol of the United States. He thought bald eagles were dishonest and lazy. Franklin's choice was the turkey.

- The cost of mailing a letter in the United States used to be paid by the person to whom it was mailed, not by the sender of the letter.

- A popular drinking song in American taverns during the early 1800s was "Anacreon in Heaven." In 1814, Francis Scott Key (1779–1843) changed the words and the song became "The Star-Spangled Banner." It was not adopted as the official anthem of the United States until 1931.

- During the 19th century, many children as young as seven years of age worked long hours in American factories.

- For ten years after the Texas Revolution in 1835, Texas was an independent country with its own president.

- "Hail to the Chief" became the official entrance music of the President of the United States during the presidency of James Polk (1845–1849). Polk was very short and "Hail to the Chief" was played so that his arrival in a room would be noticed.

- The chambers of the U.S. Congress weren't always as clean as they are today. During the 19th century, many members of the Senate and the House of Representatives chewed tobacco and spat the juice onto the carpet. Visitors were advised not to pick up anything off the floor or even look at it.

- Twenty-two people died during a huge riot involving 10,000 people that broke out at the Astor Place theater in New York

City in 1849. The dispute involved two groups of theatergoers. One group favored a production of William Shakespeare's *Macbeth* starring a British actor. The other group favored a rival production of the same play starring an American actor.

- David Rice Atchison (1807–1886) was President of the United States for one day. Atchison was the leader of the U.S. Senate and automatically became president during the one-day interval between the end of President Polk's term on March 4, 1849, and the inauguration of President Taylor on March 5. (There was a one-day gap because March 4 was a Sunday and Taylor refused to be inaugurated on the Christian sabbath.) Atchison slept during most of that day.

- An American born in 1876 could expect to live to about age 40. An American born today can expect to live to about age 75.

- The proper name for the Statue of Liberty, which was completed in 1886, is *Liberty*

Enlightening the World. The statue's inner structure was designed by Gustave Eiffel and is very similar to his famous Eiffel Tower in Paris.

• In 1886, John Pemberton, a pharmacist in Atlanta, Georgia, concocted a new headache remedy in his backyard. His assistant accidentally added some fizzy water to the concoction. The resulting drink tasted so good that the two men sold it as a soft drink. They called it Coca-Cola after the coca leaves and cola nuts it contained.

• The first woman in history to be elected mayor of a city was Susanna Medora Salter of Argonia, Kansas. Salter didn't even know she was running for mayor until she discovered her name on the ballot on the morning of the election, April 4, 1887.

• One hundred years ago, New York City stank to high heaven. Sewers often backed up, pigs roamed the streets, and garbage was tossed everywhere. Worse, the city's horses dumped thousands of pounds of fresh manure on the ground every day.

- Tomatoes, which were once called "love apples," weren't widely consumed in the United States until about 1900. Though people elsewhere in the world ate tomatoes, Americans thought the plump red fruits were poisonous.

- The Wright Brothers' first flight on December 17, 1903, which lasted only 59 seconds, was barely mentioned in the nation's newspapers. Most people doubted that a plane could actually fly or that manned flight could ever be useful.

- Movies first became popular in the United States in the early 1900s. Many community leaders disapproved of movies, however, and policemen were often ordered to raid and padlock theaters. In 1908, all the movie theaters in New York City were shut down for a week at Christmas.

- A change to the U.S. Constitution in 1920 gave all women in the United States the right to vote. By then, women in eight states had been given the vote by their state governments. Those states were California, Colorado, Idaho, Illinois, New York, Utah, Washington, and Wyoming.

- Mount Rushmore in South Dakota has the faces of four U.S. presidents carved on it. It was originally planned to have giant stone carvings of Native American leaders and famous explorers of the American frontier.

- The nickname for Vice President of the United States is "Veep." It was coined by the ten-year-old grandson of Alben Barkley (1877–1956), who was President Truman's vice president.

- Bosco, a Labrador retriever, was elected mayor of the small California town of Sunol in 1983. He served as mayor for eleven years until he died in 1994.

*I PROMISE MORE TREES AND FIRE HYDRANTS!

- The small island of Thera in the Aegean Sea was one of the most beautiful and also one of the most dangerous places in the ancient world. A volcano on the island erupted in a monumental blast in 1628 B.C., killing all the people on the island.

- Famines that took place in 7th-century England made many people there so hopeless they committed mass suicide. Standing in groups of 40 to 50 at the edges of high ocean cliffs, they joined hands and leaped to their deaths.

- The nursery rhyme "Ring Around the Rosie" goes back to the Great Plague of London in 1664–1665, which killed 70,000 people. The line "Ring Around the Rosie" refers to the round red rash that plague victims developed. The line "We all fall down" is about victims falling down dead.

- The arrival of Europeans in North and South America was a medical calamity for the native people of both continents. The Europeans brought with them unfamiliar diseases such as smallpox, measles, malaria, and pneumonia, which killed millions of Indians.

- The Great Fire of London in 1666 destroyed four-fifths of the walled city in a matter of just four days.

- On December 16, 1811, a huge earthquake struck the American Midwest. The quake whipped the Mississippi River into a frenzy and made it run backward. The quake also made the ground ripple like waves on a stormy sea and rang church bells as far away as Boston.

- The year 1816 is known as the Year Without a Summer. Unusually cold weather froze lakes and forced people to wear their winter woolies in July. Widespread crop failures led to food riots in France and Switzerland, and 65,000 people died of hunger and disease in Ireland.

- The world's worst flood happened in the fall of 1887. China's Yellow River overflowed 70-foot-high levees, drowning 900,000 people and making another 2 million homeless.

- Fourteen years before the *Titanic* sank in the Atlantic Ocean on a cold April night in 1912, an American writer named Morgan Robertson wrote a novel called *Futility*. The novel is about a giant cruise ship that hit an iceberg in the Atlantic one cold April night. The name of the cruise ship in the novel is *Titan*.

• In the spring of 1902, small eruptions of the volcano Mount Pelee on the Caribbean island of Martinique sent more than 100 six-foot-long snakes fleeing their homes on the mountainside. The snakes slithered into the town of Saint Pierre and killed 50 people and 200 animals. Shortly after, the volcano exploded, destroying Saint Pierre in just three minutes.

- A fierce tiger killed 436 people between 1902 and 1907 in the Champawat district of India.

- "The world's greatest single disaster" is what historians have called the flu epidemic that swept around the world in 1918–1919, killing 20 million to 40 million people.

- In 1919, a huge iron tank of warm molasses burst in Boston. Two million gallons of the sticky black liquid roared down the streets, drowning 21 people and injuring 150 others.

- The spectacular Tacoma Narrows Bridge in Washington state had only been open for four months in 1940 when a strong wind made it start bucking up and down like a crazed bronco. When the bucking died down, the huge suspension bridge started twisting wildly in the wind until it broke into pieces and collapsed into the waves of Puget Sound.

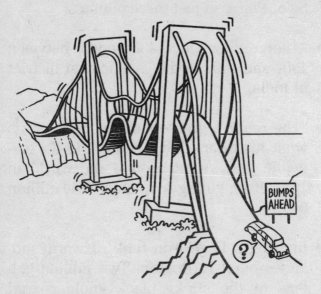

BUMPS AHEAD

- On the foggy, drizzly morning of July 28, 1945, a B-25 bomber accidentally crashed into the Empire State Building in New York City. Because the day was Saturday, only a small number of people were killed or injured. But the crash left a huge hole in the skyscraper and broke the cables of one elevator, causing it to plunge more than 75 floors to the basement. Remarkably, the elevator's operator, Betty Lou Oliver, survived the plunge.

ROUGH LANDING ON THE 94TH FLOOR

- On December 5, 1952, a heavy fog fell on London, England, and mixed with smoke from factories and household fires. The resulting smog was so thick it stopped traffic and invaded buildings. Eight thousand people and 4,000 animals choked to death on the killer smog.

- The Indus Valley civilization was one of the world's first four great civilizations. (The other three developed in Sumer, Egypt, and China.) It began about 2500 B.C. in what is now Pakistan. It ended 500 years later, probably because the Indus River shifted course, depriving the people of water for their crops.

- The Olmec Indians developed in 1200 B.C. what historians believe was the first civilization in the Americas. The Olmecs lived in Central America and built large earthen pyramids and colossal carved-stone heads that weighed as much as 36,000 pounds each.

- The earliest known histories were written in China sometime before 1000 B.C.

- Doctors in ancient India used giant ants to close up wounds made during surgery. Placed side by side along a wound, the ants would clamp the wound shut with their jaws, enabling it to heal.

- The world's first Christian empire, the Byzantine empire, began in 330 and lasted more than 1,100 years. Its capital city was Constantinople, which is now Istanbul, Turkey. Any man was eligible to become emperor and many achieved that goal by murdering the person who was then emperor.

- The Islamic religion was founded by the prophet Muhammed 1,400 years ago in the city of Mecca, in what is now Saudi

Arabia. After Muhammed died in 632, his followers waged holy wars and swiftly built a huge empire stretching all the way from Spain to India.

- Elvis Presley and the Beatles were not history's first pop music stars. In Mecca, during the 7th century, women idolized beautiful long-haired young men who sang love songs with exotic melodies.

- The Mayans of ancient Mexico thought crossed eyes were attractive. They hung beads in front of their children's faces to make the kids develop crossed eyes.

- A wandering tribe in India began moving westward to Europe sometime around the year 1000. When they reached England 500 years later, the English thought the wanderers were from Egypt and called them *Egipcyans*, a word that was later shortened to Gypsies.

- The world's oldest restaurant is Ma Yu Ching's Bucket Chicken House in the Chi-

nese city of Kaifeng. It opened in 1153 and
is still serving cheap, tasty chow today.

- A tabby cat is one with a patterned coat of
  several colors. The word tabby comes
  from Attabiya, a suburb of Baghdad that
  was famous 800 years ago for its multi-
  colored fabrics.

- Timbuktu is a small city in the African
  country of Mali. From the 1400s to the
  1700s, Timbuktu was fabulously wealthy
  and a center for higher learning. Citizens
  valued books as much as they did gold,
  and some 25,000 students attended the
  university there.

- Chinese judges wore the first sunglasses
  more than 500 years ago. The judges wore
  the smoke-colored quartz lenses to hide
  the expressions in their eyes while a trial
  was underway.

- Until his dying day, Christopher Colum-
  bus (1451–1506) refused to believe he had
  discovered a new continent. He always

believed that he had reached his original destination, India.

- The center of the great Aztec civilization was the city of Tenochtitlan, which stood on a group of islands in Lake Texcoco, Mexico, 500 years ago. It was a magnificent city, more impressive than any European city of the time, filled with temples, palaces, fountains, markets, and huge pyramids.

- The Aztecs practiced brutal religious rituals, such as tearing out the hearts and cutting off the heads of living victims. At the dedication of the great pyramid of Tenochtitlan, 20,000 people were sacrificed to the Aztec gods.

- From 1636 to 1854, the people of Japan had almost no contact with the outside world because their leaders feared Christian missionaries and European armies. No Japanese were allowed to travel abroad and only a few foreign traders were allowed into the country.

- The country of Australia began as the world's biggest jail. The first Europeans to settle on the island-continent were the English, who shipped 160,000 men and women criminals there between 1788 and 1868.

- A coup d'etat is a sudden violent overthrow of a government by a small group of people. Since it became a sovereign country in 1825, the South American country of Bolivia has had more than 190 coups.

- In 1893, New Zealand became the first nation on earth to give women the right to vote.